THE BRAINIAC'S BOOK OF THE

CLIMATE AND WEATHER

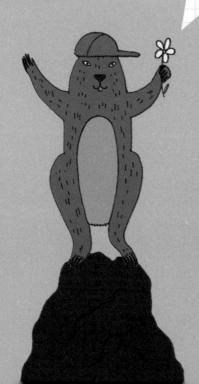

Welcome young brainiac!
I'm a groundhog. Follow me to discover
the weirdest and most wonderful facts
about the climate and weather.
How could a groundhog possibly
know about such things?
Turn to page 35 to find out!

THE BRAINIAC'S BOOK OF THE

CLIMATE AND WEATHER

ROSIE COOPER

ILLUSTRATED BY
HARRIET RUSSELL

WHAT'S INSIDE?

CLIMATE OR WEATHER?

SAME THING, RIGHT? WRONG! TUNE IN FOR THE LOWDOWN...

WEATHER is what's happening **RIGHT NOW**, and there's more on its way **TOMORROW**. Weather can change minute by minute, or hour by hour, and from **DAY TO DAY**.

THIS MORNING WILL BE SUNNY WITH A FEW SCATTERED SHOWERS. STRONG WINDS WILL BUILD FROM THE EAST, BRINGING HAIL AND SNOW, WITH THE ODD TORNADO.

SOMETHING IN THE AIR...

Weather is all about what is going on in the AIR, or atmosphere. Air can be warm or cool, dry or wet, windy or still—or a combination of these.

WATER in the air could form fog, mist, rain, hail, sleet or snow.

RAIN

HAIL

SLEET

SNOW

WHAT'S THE CLIMATE LIKE TODAY?

ASK ME AGAIN IN THIRTY YEARS...

CLIMATE is the pattern of weather in a particular place over **SEASONS** or **DECADES**. There may be very hot years, or very wet years, but the average temperature and rainfall over **30 YEARS** or more tells us about the climate.

BREAKING NEWS!
IN A FEW PARTS OF THE WORLD, WINTERS HAVE BEEN GETTING COLDER. BUT RECORDS SHOW THAT ALMOST ALL PLACES ARE GETTING WARMER.

Different places on Earth have different climates. There are warm, wet, dry, cold and hot climates.

>>> **FLIP FORWARD** to pages 12–13 to find out how **EARTH'S CLIMATE** is changing

WHAT ARE THE
REASONS FOR SEASONS?

The answer lies in the wonky world and its soggy middle!

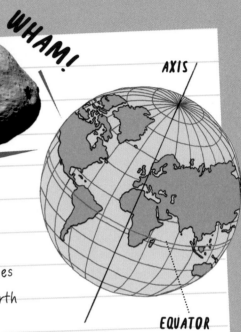

WHAM!

AXIS

EQUATOR

NEED TO KNOW FACTS

4.5 billion years ago a Mars-sized
space rock crashed into Earth, making it tilt.
Without the tilt there would be no changes
in temperature and light—so no seasons!

AXIS = the imaginary line running through the North and South poles

EQUATOR = the imaginary line running around the middle of the Earth

THE EARTH TRAVELS AROUND THE SUN ONCE A YEAR.

It is **SUMMER** in the part
tilted towards the Sun.

It is **WINTER** in the
part that is tilted away.

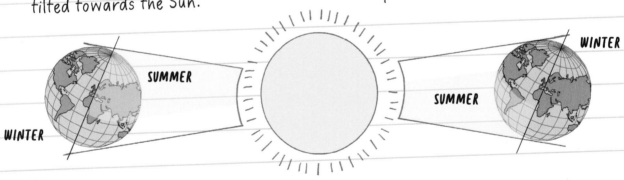

SUMMER

WINTER

WINTER

SUMMER

WHY DO BANANAS
USE SUNSCREEN?

BECAUSE THEY PEEL.

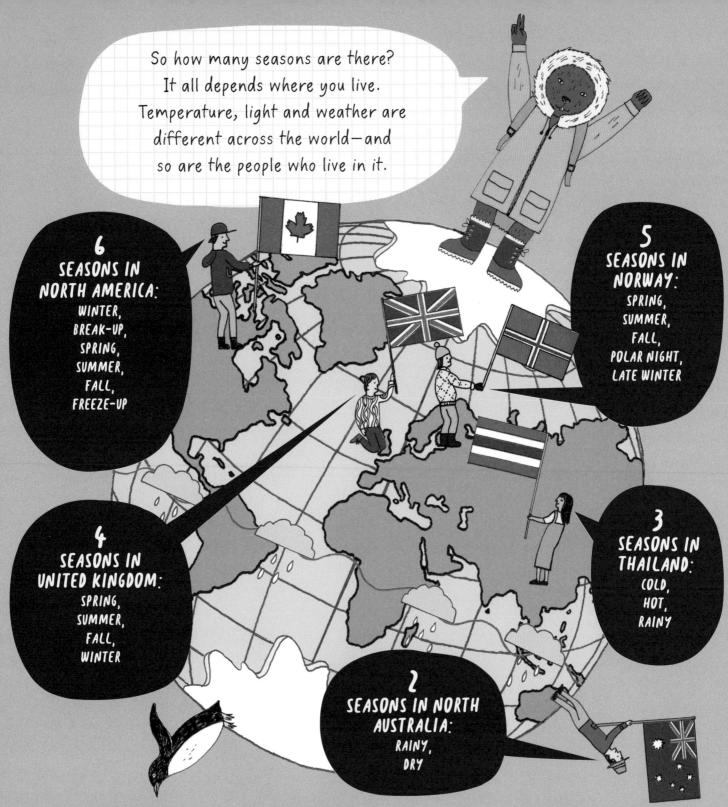

So how many seasons are there? It all depends where you live. Temperature, light and weather are different across the world—and so are the people who live in it.

6 SEASONS IN NORTH AMERICA: WINTER, BREAK-UP, SPRING, SUMMER, FALL, FREEZE-UP

5 SEASONS IN NORWAY: SPRING, SUMMER, FALL, POLAR NIGHT, LATE WINTER

4 SEASONS IN UNITED KINGDOM: SPRING, SUMMER, FALL, WINTER

3 SEASONS IN THAILAND: COLD, HOT, RAINY

2 SEASONS IN NORTH AUSTRALIA: RAINY, DRY

SOGGY MIDDLE

It is always warm near the equator, but a wiggly band of rain around the middle of the planet creates **WET** and **DRY SEASONS**.

COLD POLES

Weak sunshine at the top and bottom of the world means that the polar regions experience **EXTREME WINTERS**, with no daylight at all.

ALL FOUR

Only places that are not near the equator have **FOUR DISTINCT SEASONS**.

DATA DUMP

HOME SWEET HOME

We humans can make ourselves at home in any climate.

HOMES THAT DIG IN, RISE UP AND FLOAT ON OUR GLOBE

In very **HOT CLIMATES,** people hide from the sizzling sun in homes that don't heat up.

CAVES ROCK!

In Turkey, these multistory caves were dug out of the rock hundreds of years ago. They have been lived in ever since.

In **WET CLIMATES** where the land is low, homes are at risk from flooding.

HIGH AND DRY

In tropical Thailand, stilt houses stay dry during high tides and heavy rain.

COOL!

In Iran, tall chimneys, called windcatchers channel refreshing breezes into the home.

Floating homes in the Netherlands rise up with the flood water.

In the **FREEZING ARCTIC**, Inuit people make temporary shelters called igloos from building blocks of snow.

Many animals that hibernate through the winter sleep under the snow. The cold snow keeps them cozy because tiny pockets of trapped air between the snowflakes stop heat from escaping. That's how fluffy sweaters work, too!

CHILL OUT!

Body heat alone can keep an igloo warm. As the ice blocks heat up they melt slightly, then refreeze filling in all the gaps and protecting you from the icy wind.

An igloo warmed by body heat can keep you about 104°F warmer than outside.

In the **FUTURE**, as the climate changes, we will need new homes that use less energy and protect us from rising seas and extreme weather...

Dome homes in the U.S. are built to survive hurricane season. The wind flows around the smooth sides.

YOU LIVE IN A GREENHOUSE

NOT A LITTLE GLASS ONE, BUT A GIANT GAS ONE!

It's true! An invisible blanket of gases surrounds Earth, trapping the Sun's energy and warming the surface. They are called **GREENHOUSE GASES** and without them Earth would be freezing cold!

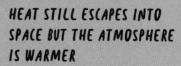

HEAT STILL ESCAPES INTO SPACE BUT THE ATMOSPHERE IS WARMER

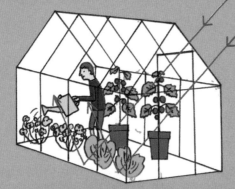

A GLASSHOUSE LETS SUNLIGHT IN AND TRAPS THE HEAT

GREENHOUSE GASES TRAP THE SUN'S ENERGY AND WARM THE EARTH'S SURFACE

JUST RIGHT

For hundreds of millions of years the natural heat-trapping gases on Earth made it warm enough for plants, animals and eventually people to survive.

TOO HOT

For the past 200 years humans have created extra greenhouse gases and these are now rapidly warming the surface of the Earth.

BURNING UP

One of the main greenhouse gases is **CARBON DIOXIDE**, or **CO_2** for short. Heat-trapping CO_2 is released when we burn forests and the fuels that power our world.

OIL is made into gas and diesel, which power vehicles.

COAL is burned in power stations.

TREES are cleared and burned for farming.

NATURAL GAS is used for cooking and heating homes.

PREHISTORIC POWER

Oil, coal and gas are called **FOSSIL FUELS**. This is because they are made from the remains of prehistoric plants and animals buried deep underground millions of years ago!

Fossil fuels take millions of years to form, but we are using them up fast, and the CO_2 they make stays in the atmosphere for 100 years.

WHAT DO YOU CALL A FOSSILIZED DINOSAUR FART?

A BLAST FROM THE PAST!

TRY THIS

THE SCIENCE OF
MAKING GASES

FARTING PLANTS AND FIZZING GAS BOMBS!

BRAINIAC HACK: SWAPPING GASES

Living things are constantly making and trading gases—in fact, you are doing it right now!

Animals and people need **OXYGEN** to live.
We breathe it in and breathe out **CARBON DIOXIDE**.

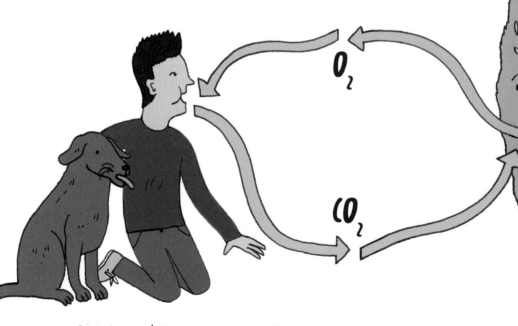

O_2

CO_2

Plants and trees are greenhouse gas-guzzlers.
They take in **CARBON DIOXIDE** from the air to make their food,
then let out the waste gas **OXYGEN**—a bit like a plant fart!

GUESS WHAT?
CARBON DIOXIDE IS USED TO KEEP FOOD FRESH AND TO MAKE DRINKS FIZZY!

SEE A PLANT FART

Pick a leaf from a tree. Put it in a shallow glass container filled with water.

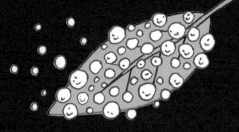

Hold the leaf down with a pebble and leave it in the sun for a few hours.

Little bubbles will start to appear on the leaf.

EXPLANATION:
The bubbles are filled with oxygen—the waste gas that has been released by the leaf. It's possible to see the gas bubbles because the leaf is under water. Pardon me!

TOOT!

EXPLODE A FIZZ BOMB

Put 3 teaspoons of baking soda on some toilet paper. Fold the paper over to make a packet.

Put 10 tablespoons (1/2 cup) of vinegar into a sealable sandwich bag.

Half seal the bag, drop in the baking soda packet and finish sealing the top, making sure there are no gaps.

Shake the bag, then stand back. Watch it puff up, fizz and POP!

THIS CAN BE MESSY! DO IT OUTSIDE, OR IN A BATH OR SINK.

EXPLANATION:
Vinegar and baking soda react when they are mixed together and make carbon dioxide gas. When the bag is full of gas, it explodes!

15

DATA DUMP

DEADLY FARTS (AND BURPS AND POOP)

Grass-grazing beasts make a powerful gas which heats up the planet.

METHANE: THE FARTY FACTS AND WAYS TO FIX IT

Cows, sheep and goats make methane gas in their stomachs when they digest food. It's a greenhouse gas which is 25 times stronger than CO_2. Cows belch and blast so much methane that it adds to global warming!

90% of the methane released by cows comes out as burps. **10%** comes from farts and poop.

Every cow burps and farts up to **79 GALLONS OF METHANE** each day. (That's enough gas to fill 26 party balloons!)

Cows can be **DANGEROUS**! In January 2014 a barn in Germany exploded. Static electricity caused methane from the farts, burps and manure of 90 cows to explode.

Earth is home to **1 BILLION COWS**. (That's one cow for every seven people.)

16

Cutting methane is one way to **STOP CLIMATE CHANGE.**

SAVE OUR EARTH

Adding **SEAWEED** to a cow's food could cut the amount of methane emitted by the cow by up to 80%.

THANK YOU!

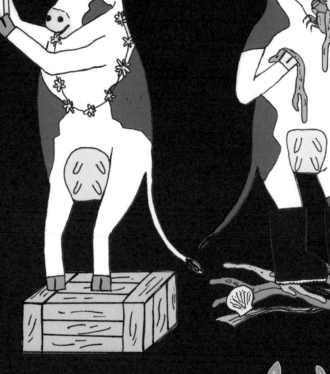

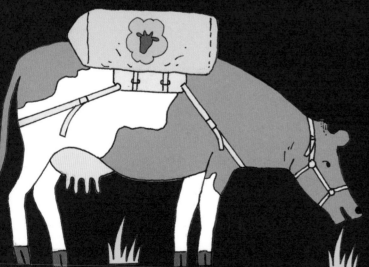

Inflatable **FARTPACKS** can collect methane from a cow's stomach. The gas is then turned into **FUEL** to run a car!

The best way to cut methane from cows is to **EAT LESS BEEF.** (Less meat means fewer methane-making cows.)

IT'S GETTING HOT IN HERE

BE A COOL CLIMATE CRUSADER

YOU DON'T NEED TO BE A SUPERHERO TO SAVE THE PLANET

By encouraging adults to reduce their energy use, changing what they buy and eat, and throwing less away, you can help reduce greenhouse gases and make the Earth cooler and cleaner. Can you find all the climate crusaders and spot people being wasteful?

CHARITY

Turn to page 62 for all the answers and more ideas on how to be a Climate Crusader

ANCIENT ICE

DISCOVER EARTH'S CHILLY PAST

NORTH POLE (ARCTIC)

EARTH TODAY

SOUTH POLE (ANTARCTIC)

Earth is 4.6 billion years old and it has seen lots of climate changes. There were warm times when crocodiles soaked up the sun in what is now the Arctic. There were also freezing times, called **ICE AGES**, when **ICE SHEETS** covered large parts of the planet.

As we still have ice at the poles all year round, we are living in an **INTERGLACIAL PERIOD** right now. A lot of the ice in Antarctica is millions of years old, and some is over **9,843 FEET THICK**.
(That's taller than nine Eiffel Towers stacked together!)

9,843 FT

6,562 FT

3,281 FT

FROZEN IN TIME

BRRRR!

2.4 BILLION YEARS AGO
The Earth was like a giant snowball. Ice may have stretched from the Poles all the way to the equator.

22,000 YEARS AGO
Northern parts of the U.S. where big cities now stand would have been buried under thick ice.

<<< FLIP BACK to page 13 to find out more about CO_2

CLIMATE CLUES

Antarctic ice is filled with tiny **AIR BUBBLES** that have been trapped for hundreds of thousands of years. Scientists study the amount of CO_2 in the ancient air to discover what Earth's climate was like in the past.

We can learn about extinct animals from ancient ice, too. Woolly mammoths from the Ice Age have been found in Russia with fur, flesh and blood, frozen solid!

TINY BUBBLES OF ANCIENT AIR

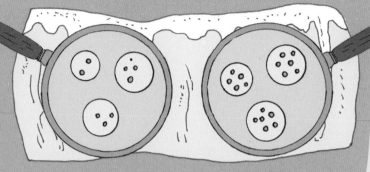

LOW CO_2 =
EARTH WAS COOLER

HIGH CO_2 =
EARTH WAS WARMER

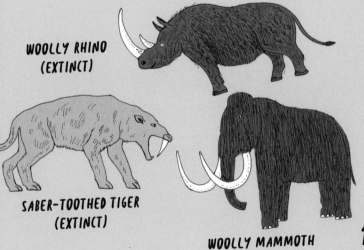

WOOLLY RHINO
(EXTINCT)

SABER-TOOTHED TIGER
(EXTINCT)

WOOLLY MAMMOTH
(EXTINCT)

11,500 YEARS AGO

This was when the last ice age came to an end. The huge, hairy, scary mammals that had roamed the planet died out.

1300 TO 1850 was the LITTLE ICE AGE

It was a time of extra cold winters in North America and Europe. In Great Britain and the Netherlands, frozen rivers and canals made great ice rinks!

WHAT'S THIS WHITE STUFF?

WHEN FREEZING WATER TURNS INTO SOMETHING EXCITING!

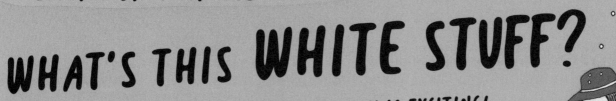

FANTASTIC FLAKES

SNOW is made from freezing water droplets high up in the clouds. At the center of every snowflake is a speck...

A SPECK OF DUST OR POLLEN

WATER STICKS TO THE SPECK

THE WATER FREEZES AND FORMS CRYSTALS

AS THE SNOWFLAKE FALLS, WATER DROPLETS IN THE AIR FREEZE ONTO IT AND MORE CRYSTALS FORM

WHEN IT LANDS, AIR TRAPPED BETWEEN THE FLAKES MAKE SNOW LIGHT AND FLUFFY

In 1885, Wilson Bentley took the first photos of snowflakes. He attached a huge camera to a microscope, caught the flakes, then held his breath to stop them from melting!

EACH SNOWFLAKE HAS 6 POINTS, BUT EVERY SINGLE ONE IS DIFFERENT!

GREAT BALLS OF ICE

HAIL is a chunk of ice that can form during a thunderstorm.

RAINDROPS ARE SUCKED UP INTO THE FREEZING CLOUD

ICE FORMS AROUND THE RAINDROPS

THEY GO ROUND AND ROUND GATHERING MORE LAYERS OF ICE

WHEN THE HAIL GETS TOO HEAVY IT FALLS TO THE GROUND

IF YOU BREAK OPEN A BIG HAILSTONE YOU CAN SEE THE LAYERS OF ICE.

The heaviest hailstones on record fell in Bangladesh in April 1986. They weighed up to 2.2 lbs. That's as much as a pineapple. Ouch!

BONK!

23

DATA DUMP

ON THE GO IN SNOW

People have been gliding around on snow for thousands of years.

WRAP UP WARM AND TAKE A SLIPPERY TRIP THROUGH TIME...

People in the **STONE AGE** skied, but not for fun. Rock paintings show **SKIERS** with just one pole. They needed the other hand for hunting!

Early skiers tied animal furs to the bottom of their skis to give them grip when they were hiking uphill. Luckily for me we have chairlifts now!

VIKING WARRIORS strapped on skis to cross their snow-covered land in times of war.

Native Americans wore **SNOWSHOES** so they could trek across deep snow. The huge shoes spread their weight, stopping them from sinking.

In snowy parts of North America in the 1920s, mail was delivered by **SNOWBIRDS**—Ford cars outfitted with tracks and skis.

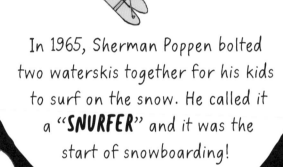

In 1965, Sherman Poppen bolted two waterskis together for his kids to surf on the snow. He called it a **"SNURFER"** and it was the start of snowboarding!

SNOWMOBILES are the modern way to whizz around on snow. In 1959, a snowmobile went on sale in Canada called a Ski-Dog, but a spelling mistake in the ad meant they became known as Ski-Doos!

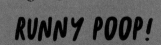

RUNNY POOP!

Sled dogs learn how to do their business on the run so the sled doesn't have to slow down!

WHERE DOES RAIN COME FROM?

Rainwater falls down from the sky—but how does it get up there?

NEED TO KNOW FACTS

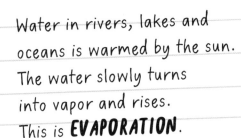

You never see rain heading to the sky. That's because it drifts up as an invisible gas, called **WATER VAPOR**.

Water in rivers, lakes and oceans is warmed by the sun. The water slowly turns into vapor and rises. This is **EVAPORATION**.

Plants give off water too. Water passes through the plant and turns into water vapor when it reaches the surface of the leaves. This is **TRANSPIRATION**.

The atmosphere gets cooler the higher you go, so water vapor cools as it rises. The vapor turns back into tiny liquid water drops, forming clouds. This is **CONDENSATION**.

When the droplets in the clouds get too big they fall as **RAIN** and their journey begins again!

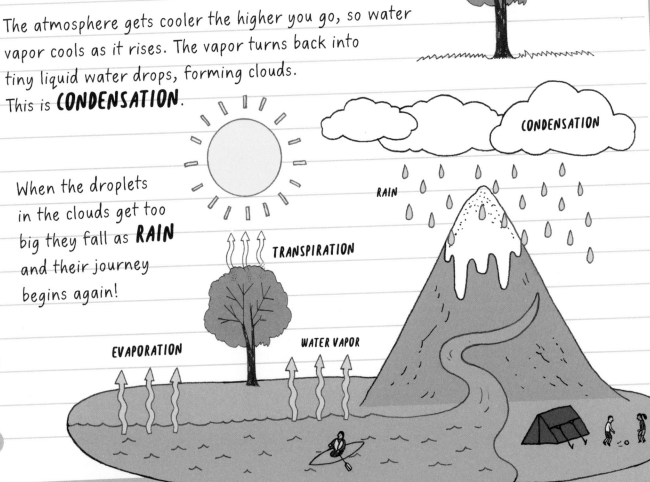

CONDENSATION

RAIN

TRANSPIRATION

EVAPORATION

WATER VAPOR

Earth has been recycling water
for over 4 billion years.
You are drinking the same water
that dinosaurs, woolly mammoths
and the first humans drank.

Take a sip of water and think about this—every single drop has been on Earth for 4 billion years, being recycled again and again. Gulp!

The Dry Valleys in Antarctica are the driest place on Earth. It never rains there.

Only 1% of the planet's water is fresh water that we can use. The rest is salty ocean water, ice, snow, water vapor or water that has soaked into the ground.

WHAT'S THE DIFFERENCE BETWEEN A HORSE AND THE WEATHER?

ONE IS REINED UP, THE OTHER RAINS DOWN!

27

CAN WATER CLIMB?

YES! WATCH THIS GRAVITY-DEFYING FEAT IN ACTION:

BRAINIAC HACK: HOW PLANTS DRINK

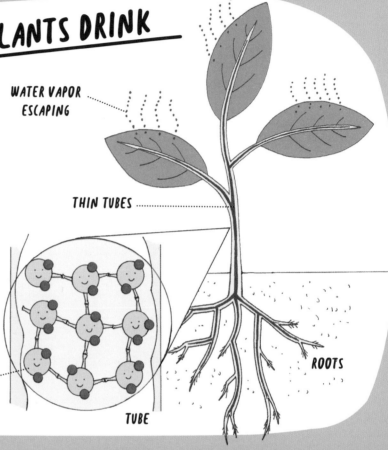

Water climbs from a plant's roots to its leaves by **CAPILLARY ACTION**.

Water can flow up the **THIN TUBES** inside a plant because its molecules are **STICKY**. They stick to the sides of the tubes and to each other. Where one molecule goes, the others follow.

WATER VAPOR ESCAPING

THIN TUBES

WATER MOLECULES BEING STICKY

TUBE

ROOTS

TRY THIS

PSYCHEDELIC CELERY

Fill a jar with water and add 1 teaspoon of food coloring.

Put a stick of leafy celery in the jar overnight.

The next day the celery leaves will have changed color.

LIQUID MAGIC

Take 2 glasses. Add water and food coloring to one.

Fold a paper towel into a narrow strip. Place one end in the colored water and the other end in the empty glass.

The empty glass starts to magically fill with water!

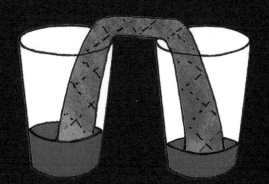

EXPLANATION:
You can actually see capillary action taking place! The water sticks to the fibers of the paper towel and travels along it.

EXPLANATION:
The water flows up to fill the tiny tubes inside the leaves, changing their color. It works with white flowers too!

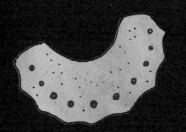

Cut the stem in half. Can you see colored dots? These are the tubes that the water flows up.

CLOUD-SPOTTER SCHOOL

THE FACTS YOU NEED TO EXCEL IN CLOUD CLASS

At any time, around 2/3 of the Earth is covered by clouds. They play a big part in our climate, so here's a crash course.

HIGH CLOUDS CAN TRAP THE HEAT AND WARM THE EARTH

HEAT

LOW CLOUDS BLOCK THE SUN AND COOL THE EARTH

HEAT

CLOUD CHEMISTRY

Clouds are **WATER DROPLETS** mixed with specs of **DUST** and **AIR**.

Height and temperature make clouds different shapes and sizes.

F-F-FREEZING

HIGH clouds are made of ice. Strong winds give them a wispy edge.

MIDDLE clouds are made of water droplets and tiny bits of ice.

AIR GETS COLDER HIGHER UP IN THE SKY

LOW clouds are made of water droplets. They often have a sharp outline.

NOT TOO COLD

There are 10 cloud types, and their names come from combinations of five Latin* words.

LEARN YOUR LATIN

*Latin is a very old language that is used to name things in nature.

LATIN WORD	MEANING	DESCRIPTION
CUMULUS	PILE OR HEAP	PUFFY, LIKE SCOOPS OF ICE CREAM
STRATUS	LAYER OR COVER	LOW SHEETS ACROSS THE SKY
CIRRUS (CIRRO)	CURL OF HAIR	WISPY, LIKE COTTON CANDY
NIMBUS (NIMBO)	RAIN CLOUD	LOW, FLAT AND GRAY
ALTUM (ALTO)	HEIGHT	A WORD FOR MID-LEVEL CLOUDS

Clouds were given their Latin names over 200 years ago. What five words would you use to name the clouds today?

TEST YOURSELF

Can you name the clouds you see on different days? Try to spot all 10!

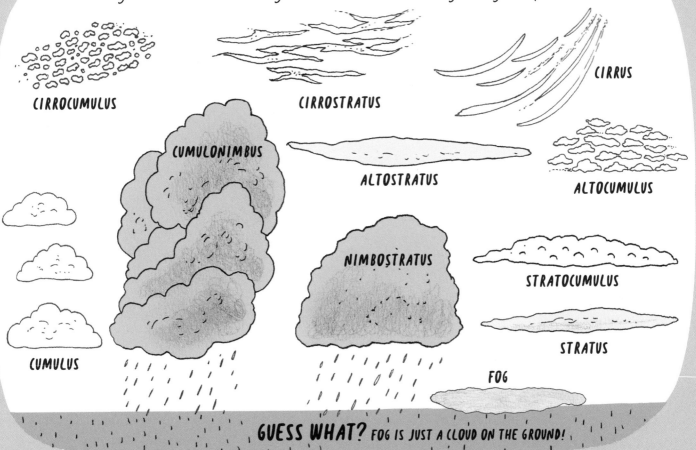

CIRROCUMULUS

CIRROSTRATUS

CIRRUS

CUMULONIMBUS

ALTOSTRATUS

ALTOCUMULUS

NIMBOSTRATUS

STRATOCUMULUS

CUMULUS

STRATUS

FOG

GUESS WHAT? FOG IS JUST A CLOUD ON THE GROUND!

DATA DUMP HEAD IN THE CLOUDS

Keep your eyes on the sky—there's some weird stuff going on!

OUT-OF-THIS-WORLD CLOUDS AND SUPER POWERS:

CAP CLOUDS hover above chilly mountain peaks like winter hats.

It's a flying saucer! Many UFO sightings may just be cosmic **LENTICULAR CLOUDS**.

Mmmm! Lovely, bubbly, melty **MAMMATUS CLOUD**. It looks good enough to eat!

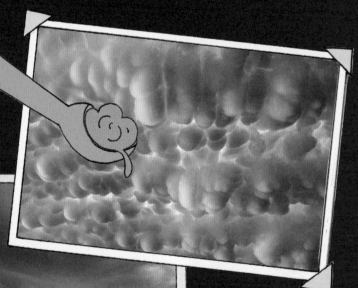

The bad weather has been packed up in this **ROLL CLOUD** for the day.

Grab a board and surf the sky on a **KELVIN–HELMHOLTZ WAVE**

FALLSTREAK HOLES punch big spyholes in the sky.

Some people believe they can make clouds vanish, shrink or grow using a mind power called **CLOUD PSYCHOKINESIS**. As fun as this might sound, it has no scientific basis whatsoever, so don't try this in a storm!

WHAT DO YOU SEE?

If it's a rabbit, you might have **PAREIDOLIA**. Don't worry, it's not serious. It's when people see shapes, animals and faces in clouds, objects, buildings—and just about everything!

Yikes! A monster mushroom **SUPERCELL** storm cloud is heading this way!

FORECASTING CLASS

THERE'S AN INVISIBLE FORCE AT WORK...

You can't see it or feel it, but the weight of the air is pressing down on you. This is called **AIR PRESSURE**. The amount of air pressure goes up and down, bringing changes in the weather.

HIGH PRESSURE WILL MOVE IN, BRINGING SUNSHINE FOR THE WEEKEND.

These lines on a weather map show the air's temperature and pressure.

COOL AIR AND HIGH PRESSURE = FINE WEATHER

WARM AIR AND LOW PRESSURE = RAINFALL

HIGHS AND LOWS

When cool air sinks it gets squashed and causes **HIGH PRESSURE**. This squashing warms the air so there's no condensation.

HIGH PRESSURE

When warm air rises it spreads out and causes **LOW PRESSURE**. Spreading out cools the air, creating condensation and rainfall.

LOW PRESSURE

HOW CAN YOU PREDICT THE WEATHER?

IF YOU DON'T HAVE A SUPERCOMPUTER...
...look to nature for the answer.

Birds singing in the rain means better weather is coming soon.

USE A SUPERCOMPUTER!
Weather forecasters use basic equations and a supercomputer to predict the weather forecast you hear on TV.

Bees and butterflies can't fly in rain. If they buzz off grab a raincoat.

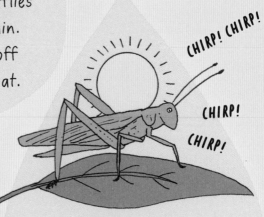

A cricket's chirps speed up as the weather warms up. Count the chirps in 15 seconds and then add 37 to get the temperature in °F.

On a dry day a pine cone's scales open out. On a wet day they close up.

Daisy petals close up if rain is on the way.

WAKE A GROUNDHOG
This North American animal sleeps in its burrow all winter.

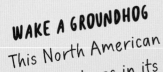

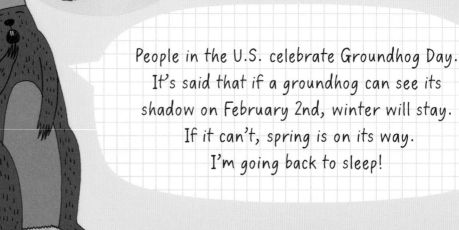

People in the U.S. celebrate Groundhog Day. It's said that if a groundhog can see its shadow on February 2nd, winter will stay. If it can't, spring is on its way. I'm going back to sleep!

WEATHER-COMBATING WEAPONS

Uncover the history of sun and rain self-defense.

NEED TO KNOW FACTS

4,000 years ago **UMBRELLAS** were cool.
That's because ancient Egyptians and Greeks used them
as sun shades ("umbra" is the Latin word for shadow).

It's thought that Emperor Wang Mang of China
owned the first **COLLAPSIBLE UMBRELLA**.
It was made 2,000 years ago to protect him
while he rode in his carriage.

WATERPROOF UMBRELLAS
were invented in ancient China.
Paper parasols were coated
with waterproof wax and
lacquer so that the
rain ran off.

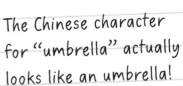

The Chinese character
for "umbrella" actually
looks like an umbrella!

WHAT HAPPENS WHEN IT RAINS CATS AND DOGS?

YOU MIGHT STEP IN A POODLE!

SHADY STORIES

In 1978, Bulgarian writer Georgi Markov was **MURDERED** in London, U.K., using poison injected by an umbrella tip. It is thought that the Russian secret police, or KGB, were to blame.

In many cultures it's **BAD LUCK** to open an umbrella indoors. In ancient Egypt people believed that opening a parasol in the shade was an **INSULT** to the sun god Amun-Ra.

In the U.K. in the 1800s, wealthy ladies had parasol purses. They carried perfume, notepaper and sometimes even a **DAGGER** in the special handle.

Every year in London nearly 75,000 umbrellas are forgotten on public transit.

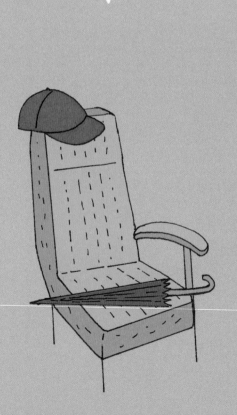

THE ART OF BENDING LIGHT

Discover the colorful science behind making rainbows.

BRAINIAC HACK: RAINBOWS

LIGHT travels in straight lines and looks white.

When light passes through **WATER** and is reflected at the back of a raindrop, it bends and separates into all its colors.

RESULT: sunlight passing through raindrops bends to make a **RAINBOW**.

WHITE LIGHT

LIGHT BENDS

WHAT YOU SEE

HOSEBOWS

Stand in the garden on a sunny day with the sun behind you.

Spray fine mist in front of you using a hose or a plant mister bottle.

EXPLANATION:
You have re-created what happens in the sky. Sunlight reflecting off the back of the water droplets is what makes a rainbow.

GUESS WHAT? YOU DON'T NEED SUN OR RAIN TO MAKE A RAINBOW!

DISHY REFLECTION

Fill a dish with water and lean a mirror half in and half out of the water.

Shine a flashlight so that the beam hits the underwater part of the mirror. Hold a piece of white paper above the mirror to see a rainbow.

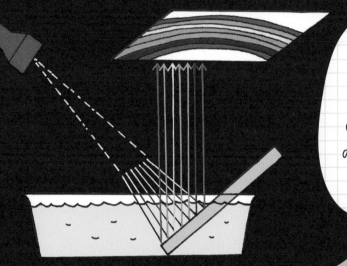

MOONBOWS
Pale rainbows can appear when moonlight travels through rain or mist.

EXPLANATION:
The beam of light from the flashlight is made up of different colors. They are split up as they enter and leave the water, making the rainbow you see on the paper.

RED ORANGE YELLOW GREEN BLUE INDIGO VIOLET

MYTH BUSTER

Mega scientist Sir Isaac Newton first proved that light is made of many colors in 1672. He counted 7 colors in the rainbow, but there are actually about 100 that we can see with our eyes!

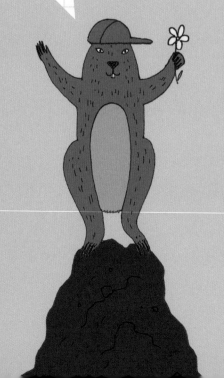

RAINING CATS AND DOGS

DATA DUMP

People around the world have many wacky ways to say "It's raining really hard"...

"DOG POOP IS FALLING"
CHINA

"TRACTORS ARE FALLING"
SLOVAKIA

"IT'S RAINING OLD WOMEN WITH KNOBKERRIES*"
SOUTH AFRICA

*a wooden club

"IT'S RAINING KNIVES AND FORKS"
WALES

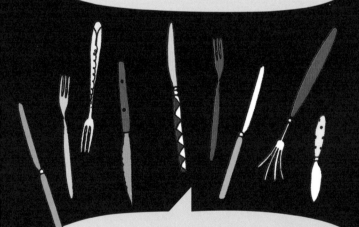

"DOGS ARE DRINKING IN THEIR NOSES"
HAITI

LET THE SUN SHINE IN
STAR POWER!

The Sun is millions and millions of times more powerful than the power we use on Earth!

NEED TO KNOW FACTS

The Sun's energy is called **SOLAR ENERGY**. Unlike gas, coal and oil it is **RENEWABLE**, which means it won't run out. It doesn't harm the planet either. Solar energy already powers some everyday gadgets and homes.

SOLAR CELLS turn sunlight into electricity. A group of solar cells is called a **SOLAR PANEL**

SOLAR PANELS face the Sun to catch the rays

Sunlight is absorbed by the **CELLS** and turned into electrical energy

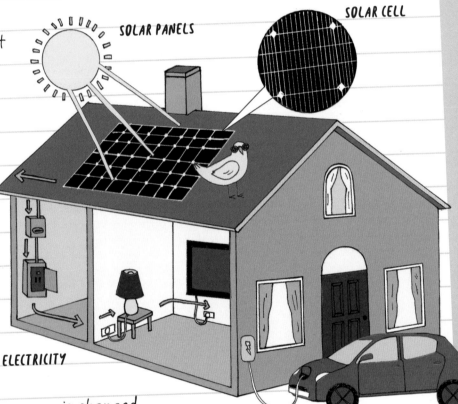

SOLAR PANELS

SOLAR CELL

ELECTRICITY

The energy is changed into **ELECTRICITY**

UM, WHO TURNED OUT THE LIGHTS?

SO WHY DON'T WE USE MORE OF THE SUN'S POWER?

The problem with solar power is that it stops being made when the sun goes down. We need much better batteries to store solar energy ready to be used at night.

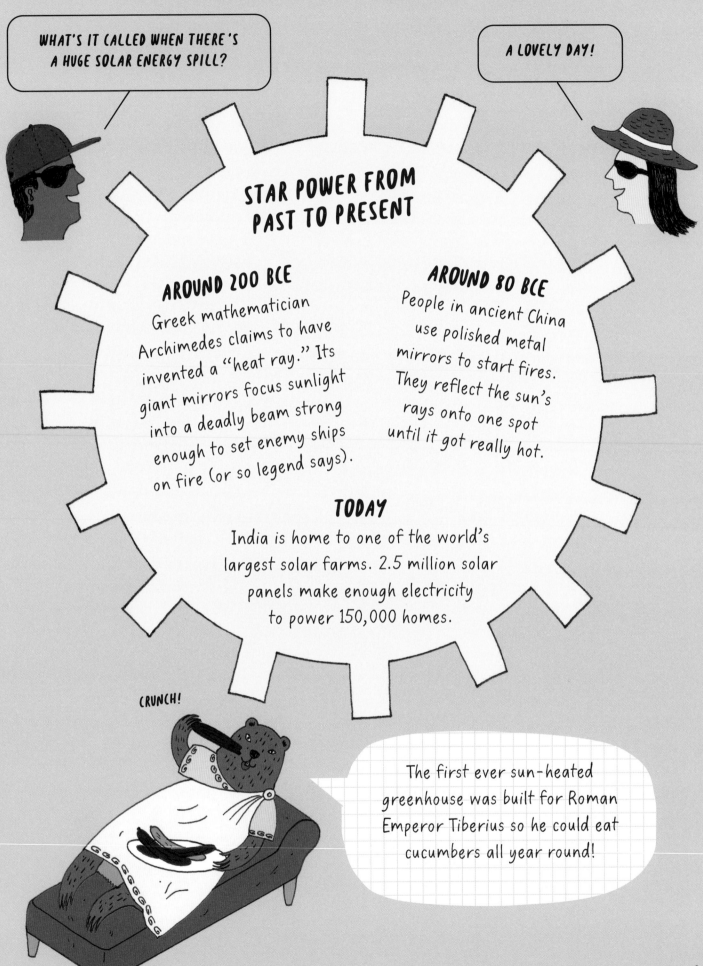

LET THE SUN SHINE IN

SO HOT RIGHT NOW

THERE'S NOTHING COOL ABOUT CLIMATE CHANGE

At different times in its life, Earth has been **HOT** and steamy or **ICY** all over! Most of these climate changes happened **SLOWLY** over millions of years, but now Earth is heating up at record speed.

200 years ago, we started burning lots of **FOSSIL FUELS**. No one knew the harm this would do. Earth's average temperature has risen by about **33.8°F** since then—and it's still going up.

STOP
GLOBAL WARMING

FEEL THE HEAT

A **33.8°F** temperature rise might seem small, but it is having a **BIG IMPACT**. We are starting to see more ...

In August 2020 the world's highest temperature was recorded in Death Valley, California: 129.9°F. That would feel like sitting next to a roaring fire in summer, dressed for winter!

- extreme weather
- rising sea levels

- droughts
- heatwaves
- wildfires
- animals and plants becoming extinct

44

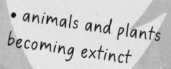

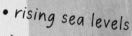

<<< FLIP BACK to page 13 to find out how **FOSSIL FUELS** heat the planet

LISTEN UP, PEOPLE!

Climate change is bad news for nature, humans and wildlife:

ELEPHANTS DRINK UP TO 61 GALLONS OF WATER A DAY—A BATHTUB-FULL. AS THE GRASSLANDS BECOME HOTTER AND DRIER, THERE IS LESS FOR THEM TO DRINK.

ASIAN ELEPHANT

TURTLES LAY THEIR EGGS IN THE SAND, BUT IF IT IS TOO WARM, ONLY THE FEMALE TURTLES HATCH.

A PUFFIN'S FAVORITE FOOD IS HERRING. AS THE OCEAN HEATS UP, THE NUMBER OF HERRING IS GOING DOWN AND THEIR CHICKS ARE STARVING.

PUFFIN

GREEN SEA TURTLE

SURVIVAL EXPERTS

COCKROACHES were scuttling around the Earth before dinosaurs even existed. These creepy critters burrow underground to protect themselves.

WE ARE THE ODD ONES OUT. BEES LOVE HOT WEATHER, BUT OUR HOMES HAVE BEEN POLLUTED. WITHOUT US TO POLLINATE PLANTS, FRUIT AND VEGETABLES CANNOT GROW—AND THERE IS LESS FOOD FOR EVERYONE.

BUMBLEBEE

>>> FLIP FORWARD to page 62 to find ways to SAVE THE PLANET

TRY THIS

BAKING HOT

Turn a pizza box into a sun-powered melting machine.

WHAT YOU NEED

- a very sunny day
- takeout pizza box
- marker
- ruler
- craft knife*
- clear plastic wrap
- sticky tape
- aluminum foil
- glue
- black paper
- a wooden skewer

WHAT TO DO

Cut a flap in the box lid*, leaving a 1.2 in. border around the edge.

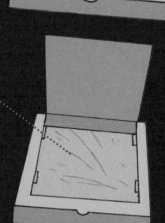

Fold the flap back along the uncut side. Tape a double layer of plastic wrap across the hole in the lid.

Glue aluminum foil to the underneath of the flap and the insides of the box.

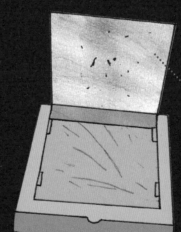

Glue a piece of black paper to the bottom. Prop the lid open with the skewer.

46   *Ask an adult to help with cutting.

MELT SOME S'MORES

Top plain cookies with a marshmallow and place on the black paper in the oven.

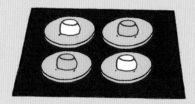

Close the clear lid tightly and set the box in the sun. Tilt the flap to reflect the light inside.

When the marshmallows have melted, add a chunk of chocolate and melt again. Finish with another cookie.

YUM!

Swiss scientist Horace Bénédict de Saussure built the first sun-powered oven in 1767. He cooked fruit in a glass box on a black table!

BRAINIAC HACK: SOLAR OVENS

A solar oven uses the sun's rays to heat food. Here's how:

Light **REFLECTS** off **SHINY** surfaces.

The **BLACK** surface gets hot because it takes in, or **ABSORBS**, more of the sun's rays than a pale surface.

The **CLEAR** lid lets sunlight through, but **TRAPS** the heat inside. (This is how a glass greenhouse heats up, too.)

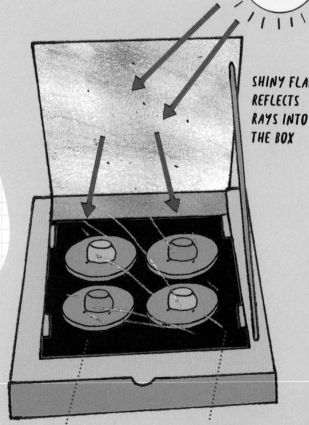

SHINY FLAP REFLECTS RAYS INTO THE BOX

BLACK SURFACE INSIDE GETS HOT

CLEAR LID LETS IN LIGHT AND TRAPS HEAT INSIDE

47

WHAT MAKES THE WIND BLOW?

IT ALL HAS TO DO WITH OUR SUNNY, SPINNING WORLD

SOAK IT UP

Wind begins with the **SUN**. Its rays heat the surface of our planet—some areas more than others. Where the surface heats up, the air heats up too. **WARM AIR** is lighter than cold air, so it **RISES**. Now air is on the move!

The seaside is often windy because the sun heats the land more quickly than the sea.

The **WARM** land heats the air above it and the air rises.

WARM AIR RISING

COOL air over the sea rushes in to fill its place—creating wind.

COOL AIR RUSHING IN

WARM LAND

COLD SEA

WHAT IS THE WIND'S FAVORITE COLOR?

BLEW!

<<< FLIP BACK to pages 34-35 to find out about AIR PRESSURE

IN A SPIN

Air and ocean currents **CURVE** as they travel across the Earth. This is because our planet is turning, or **ROTATING**.

NORTH of the equator air curves to the **RIGHT**.

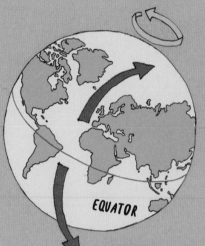

THE EQUATOR IS THE INVISIBLE LINE AROUND THE CENTER OF THE EARTH

EQUATOR

SOUTH of the equator air curves to the **LEFT**.

GIVE IT A WHIRL!

Try it out on a spinning merry-go-round. Sit across from a friend and throw a ball to them—it seems to curve away!

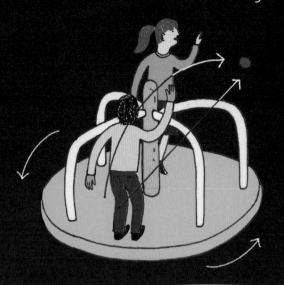

There is a myth that the bathtub empties in opposite directions in the Northern and Southern hemispheres. But the effects are too small on the scale of a bathtub.

WHIRLING WINDS

The turning Earth makes powerful winds spin too. **CYCLONES** and **HURRICANES** are huge tropical storms that spin as cool air is sucked in from all directions.

NORTH OF THE EQUATOR STORMS TURN ANTI-CLOCKWISE

SOUTH OF THE EQUATOR STORMS TURN CLOCKWISE

GUSTY GIZMO

TRY THIS

Raid the recycling to make a wind-measuring machine.

WHAT YOU NEED

- 2 strips of thick cardboard 12 in. x 2 in.
- 4 small paper cups or yogurt pots
- pencil with an eraser

- stapler
- marker

- thumbtack
- stopwatch or timer

MAKE AN ANEMOMETER

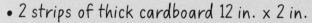

Make a cross with the strips of cardboard and staple them together in the middle.

Color in one of the cups. This makes it easier to count the spins.

Staple the cups to the ends of the cardboard cross, all pointing in the same direction.

Push the tack through the cross into the pencil eraser.

TACK PUSHED THROUGH TO ERASER

COLORED CUP

PENCIL

CUPS STAPLED TO CARDBOARD ARMS

Test your anemometer spins freely, then take it outside. Using a timer, count the spins in 10 seconds.

BRAINIAC HACK: WIND SPEED

The speed of the wind can be measured by an **ANEMOMETER**.

When the **WIND** blows, the air catches in the cups, pushing them around. The stronger the wind, the faster the cups **SPIN**.

The anemometer **COUNTS** the number of spins to calculate the wind's **SPEED**.

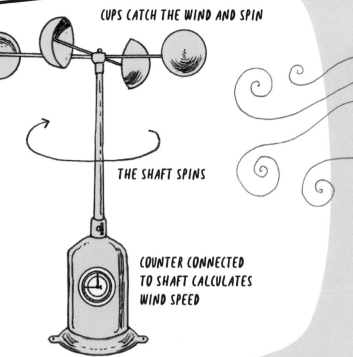

CUPS CATCH THE WIND AND SPIN

THE SHAFT SPINS

COUNTER CONNECTED TO SHAFT CALCULATES WIND SPEED

LET IT BLOW!

Measure the strength of the wind on different days and in different locations. Try up high, down low, in parks, woods and built up places.

SPINS IN 10 SECS	WIND RATING
1-5	Calm
6-10	Light breeze
11-20	Gentle breeze
21-30	Fresh breeze
31-40	Strong breeze
41 or more	Blowing a gale!

EXPLANATION:

You'll find that the wind gets stronger up high and in open spaces where there are no buildings or trees to block it.

GUESS WHAT? YOU CAN SPOT ANEMOMETERS AT AIRPORTS AND BY RAILROADS, ON BOATS AND TALL CRANES, WHERE HIGH WINDS CAN BE DANGEROUS.

CATCHING THE WIND

DATA DUMP

Wind power was important before we burned gas, oil and coal. Now it's back...

BE BLOWN AWAY BY WEIRD AND WONDERFUL WINDY INVENTIONS:

IN THE PAST...

The ancient Egyptians were the first to use **SAILING SHIPS**. They could drift downstream on the River Nile, but needed wind power to travel back against the current.

WINDMILLS were grinding grain in Iran 1,000 years ago and became popular across the world. In the Netherlands, windmills also mixed paint, sawed wood, made oil, and pumped water off flooded land.

QUACK

BAAAA

The first passenger **BALLOON FLIGHT** in 1783 carried a sheep, a duck and a cockerel! Balloons can only go where the wind blows them.

A **KITE-DRAWN CARRIAGE** called the Charvolant was invented in England in 1826. Although it was fast, it was hard to steer and the idea never took off.

PRESENT...

Modern explorers can whizz around the world in high-tech **HOT AIR BALLOONS**. The record time is 11 days!

Kite surfers use the power of the wind and the waves to reach record speeds. The aim is to jump high in the air, do tricks and stay up for as long as possible. WAHEY!

ENDLESS ENERGY

The world is turning back to fan-tastic wind power to make electricity. Wind turbines do not pollute the air or water and the wind that turns their blades will never run out.

...AND FUTURE

Wind-powered vehicles could be silently rolling along our roads in the future. There are even plans for a wind-powered Grand Prix!

Today's **CARGO SHIPS** belch out nasty fumes. One day, giant boats crammed with goods could be blown along by massive metal sails.

THE GOLDILOCKS PLANET

EARTH IS PRETTY PERFECT—EVEN IF YOU DON'T LIKE PORRIDGE!

NEED TO KNOW FACTS

Earth is a **GOLDILOCKS PLANET** because it is not too close to the Sun (too hot), or too far from the Sun (too cold). It is **JUST RIGHT** for water not to freeze and for people, groundhogs, bullfrogs and everything in between to survive!

THE PLANETS IN OUR SOLAR SYSTEM GO FROM BOILING TO F-F-F-FREEZING!

SUN

VENUS
880°F

MARS
82°F

MERCURY
800°F

EARTH
59°F

JUPITER
-162°F

URANUS
-319°F

NEPTUNE
-330°F

SATURN
-216°F

Earth is also surrounded by a blanket of gases, called the **ATMOSPHERE**. It keeps us warm and gives us oxygen to breathe.

The atmosphere has five layers. Our **WEATHER** happens in the layer closest to Earth.

WEATHER HAPPENS HERE

EXOSPHERE
THERMOSPHERE
MESOSPHERE
STRATOSPHERE
TROPOSPHERE

EARTH

GUESS WHAT?

WITHOUT OUR ATMOSPHERE THE EARTH'S AVERAGE TEMPERATURE WOULD BE -0.4°F

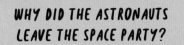

WHY DID THE ASTRONAUTS LEAVE THE SPACE PARTY?

THERE WAS NO ATMOSPHERE!

Now I know what the weather is like on other planets, I'm never going to complain about rain again!

ALIEN WEATHER

Mars has mega dust storms that cover the planet in red dust for weeks.

Saturn's largest moon, Titan, has simliar weather to Earth. Unfortunately, instead of water, it has methane—the stuff that cows burp and fart!

Jupiter's red spot is a huge storm as big as two Earths. The storm has winds of 401 miles per hour and has lasted for at least 340 years.

The distant planet COROT-7b has rock clouds which rain little pebbles!

Scientists believe it rains diamonds on Neptune. Sadly you would be frozen by the icy temperatures in seconds, so no time to become a billionaire!

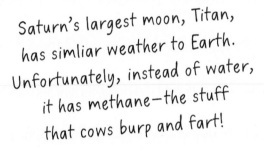

TRY THIS

BRIGHT SPARKS

Blow up a storm with a spoon, tons of sparks and bagfuls of boom!

BRAINIAC HACK: LIGHTNING

Lightning is a giant spark of **ELECTRICITY**. It forms inside storm clouds where **ICE** particles move up to the top of the cloud and **WATER** droplets sink to the bottom.

They **RUB** against each other as they pass and charge up with **STATIC ELECTRICITY**.

When the charge is strong enough, the cloud lets out energy as a bolt of **LIGHTNING**.

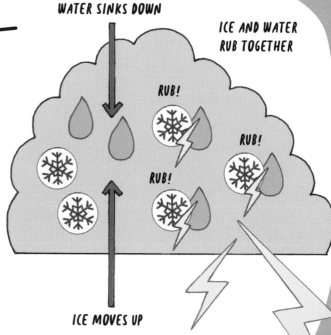

WATER SINKS DOWN

ICE AND WATER RUB TOGETHER

RUB!
RUB!
RUB!
RUB!

ICE MOVES UP

WHAT A SHOCKER!

Blow up a balloon and rub it against your hair for 2 minutes.

Turn out the lights and slowly move a metal spoon towards the balloon. You will see tiny electric sparks!

EXPLANATION:

You made static electricity by rubbing two surfaces together—just like the ice and water in the cloud. Electricity is attracted to metal, so a spark jumps from the balloon to the spoon.

56

BRAINIAC HACK: THUNDER

Thunder is the sound made by **LIGHTNING**. Lightning travels at hundreds of thousands of miles per hour and is five times hotter than the Sun! It **HEATS** the air around it so quickly that the air gets bigger. The air **EXPANDS** and **VIBRATES**, and these vibrations travel through the air until we hear them as loud **THUNDER CLAPS!**

RUMBLE!

BOOM!

THUNDER CLAPS

Get a paper bag and blow it up until it is full. Twist the top to close it.

Quickly burst the bag by clapping it with two hands. Listen for the bang!

BANG!

GUESS WHAT?
WE SEE LIGHTNING BEFORE WE HEAR THUNDER BECAUSE LIGHT TRAVELS SO MUCH FASTER THAN SOUND. WHEN THERE IS ALMOST NO GAP BETWEEN THE LIGHTNING AND THUNDER, THEN THE STORM IS JUST OVERHEAD. A DELAY BETWEEN THEM MEANS IT'S FURTHER AWAY.

EXPLANATION:
When the bag bursts, the air inside is forced out quickly and vibrates. The vibrations reach our ears as a BANG—just like the vibrating air that creates thunder claps!

57

WEIRD WEATHER

Wind, temperature and water can conjure up some tricks and treats!

PREPARE FOR FROZEN FOOD, COSMIC LIGHTS AND CREEPY CLOTHES...

DATA DUMP

MMM, FROSTED DOUGHNUTS!

SNOW DOUGHNUTS are snowballs rolled by the wind. The powdery inside gets blown away, leaving a hole.

CALL THE FIRE BRIGADE!

That's a **DUST DEVIL** not smoke. Swirling tornadoes of sand and dirt get whipped up in hot deserts.

ALIENS HAVE LANDED!

AURORAL LIGHTS do come from space. When particles from the Sun hit the gases high in the atmosphere of Earth, they glow.

THIS CLOUD IS ON THE GROUND!

That's a **HABOOB**—a mile-high sandstorm that can move at 60 miles per hour! RUN!

COOL ICE SCULPTURE!

In an **ICE STORM**, freezing rain coats everything with ice, transforming trees and cars into frozen works of art!

BRIGHT NIGHTS!

The **CATATUMBO LIGHTNING** storm rages over Lake Maracaibo in Venezuela up to 160 nights of the year. Hundreds of bolts light up the sky every hour!

In the Arctic temperatures drop to around -31°F in winter. Any clothes that are hung out to dry freeze solid in minutes. Frozen jeans can even stand up on their own!

THE SEA IS BEING SUCKED INTO THE SKY!

GLOSSARY

AIR PRESSURE
The force of the air pressing down on Earth. Air pressure changes and can be high or low.

ANEMOMETER
An instrument for measuring the strength and speed of the wind.

ATMOSPHERE
The blanket of gases that surrounds the Earth.

CARBON DIOXIDE (CO2)
The gas that is made when fossil fuels or wood are burned, or when people or animals breathe out.

CLIMATE
The weather conditions usually found in an area over a long period of time.

CLIMATE CHANGE
Changes in the world's weather caused by increased levels of heat-trapping greenhouse gases, such as carbon dioxide and methane.

CONDENSATION
When water vapor cools and turns into a tiny water droplet.

CYCLONE
A violent tropical storm that swirls around a low-pressure area.

EVAPORATION
When a liquid changes into a gas, usually by heating.

FORECAST
To predict what the weather will be like.

FOSSIL FUELS
Fuels such as gas, coal and oil, which were formed underground millions of years ago from plant and animal remains.

GAS
A substance that is like air, that is neither a solid nor a liquid.

GLOBAL WARMING
An increase in the world temperature caused by gases, like carbon dioxide, trapping heat around the Earth.

GREENHOUSE GAS
A gas that traps heat around the Earth.

HAIL
Small, hard balls of ice that fall from the sky like rain.

HURRICANE
A violent tropical storm that has a circular movement.

ICE AGE
A time in the past when the temperature was very cold and ice covered large parts of the Earth.

ICE SHEETS
A thick layer of ice that covers an area of land and does not melt.

METHANE
One of the greenhouse gases that traps heat around the Earth. Cows burp and fart methane.

OXYGEN (O2)
A gas in the air that people, animals and plants need to live.

PARASOL
A type of sunshade that is carried like an umbrella to give protection from the sun.

POLLUTION
Damage caused to the land, air or water by harmful substances.

RENEWABLE ENERGY
Energy that is produced from things that will never run out, such as the Sun, wind or moving water, rather than fuels like coal.

SLEET
Wet, partly melted falling snow.

SOLAR ENERGY
Energy collected from the light of the Sun.

TORNADO
A powerful and destructive wind that forms into a spinning cone and moves across the ground.

TRANSPIRATION
Losing water through the surface of a plant.

TURBINE
An engine that has blades that are made to turn by steam, air or water to produce electricity.

TYPHOON
A large, violent wind that moves in a circular movement.

WATER VAPOR
Water that has been heated to form an invisible gas.

WE WANT ANSWERS!

CLIMATE CRUSADER

○ The things ringed in **GREEN** show Climate Crusaders at work. Energy and water are being saved, garbage is being recycled and things are being reused.

○ Things ringed in **RED** show people being wasteful. Energy and water are being wasted, garbage is being created and the air is being polluted.

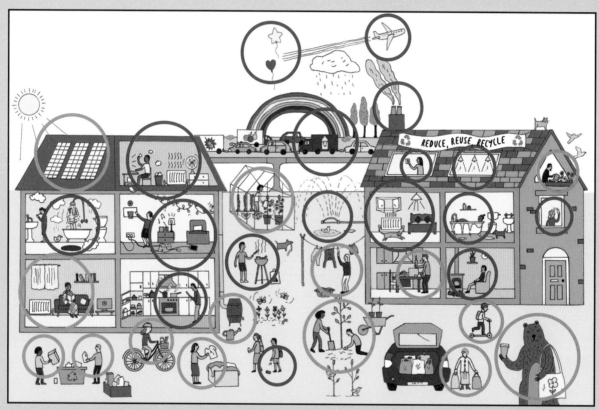

WAYS TO BE A CLIMATE CRUSADER:
- TURN OFF LIGHTS, TVS, RADIOS AND CHARGERS WHEN THEY ARE NOT IN USE
- TAKE SHORT SHOWERS AND COLLECT RAIN WATER FOR THE GARDEN
- TURN DOWN HEATERS AND WEAR MORE LAYERS
- WALK OR BIKE INSTEAD OF GOING BY CAR
- RECYCLE PAPER, PLASTIC, CARDBOARD AND TIN CANS
- BUY THINGS SECONDHAND
- GIVE THINGS YOU DON'T NEED TO CHARITY
- EAT MORE MEAT-FREE MEALS

FIND OUT MORE...
climatekids.nasa.gov/
www.amnh.org/explore/ology/climate-change
www.wwf.org.uk/learn/effects-of/climate-change
www.chrishaughton.com/antarctica

INDEX

ROSIE COOPER

is a London-based IT specialist with an MA in Geography. She is a podcast maven with a love of the great outdoors and extreme weather. This is her first book for children.

HARRIET RUSSELL

is the illustrator of over ten books for children including the bestselling *This Book Thinks You're a Scientist* published by Thames & Hudson. She lives in London.

ADAM SCAIFE

is Head of Long Range Forecasting at the Met Office and professor at Exeter University in the UK. Adam has published around 200 studies on climate science and was recently awarded the Edward Appleton Medal by the Institute of Physics and the Buchan Prize of the Royal Meteorological Society.

The Brainiac's Book of the Climate and Weather © 2022 Thames & Hudson Ltd, London
Text © 2022 Rosie Cooper
Illustrations © 2022 Harriet Russell

Edited by Cath Ard
Designed by Belinda Webster
Scientific consultant Professor Adam Scaife

First published in 2022 in the United States of America by Thames & Hudson Inc., 500 Fifth Avenue, New York, New York 10110

Library of Congress Control Number 2021933970

ISBN 978-0-500-65246-6

Printed and bound in China by RR Donnelley

MIX
Paper from responsible sources
FSC® C144853
www.fsc.org

Be the first to know about our new releases, exclusive content and author events by visiting
thamesandhudson.com
thamesandhudsonusa.com
thamesandhudson.com.au